Earthforms

Islands

by Christine Webster

Consultant:
Robert S. Anderson, PhD
Associate Professor of Geological Sciences
University of Colorado at Boulder

Capstone press
Mankato, Minnesota

Bridgestone Books are published by Capstone Press,
151 Good Counsel Drive, P.O. Box 669, Mankato, Minnesota 56002.
www.capstonepress.com

Library of Congress Cataloging-in-Publication Data
Webster, Christine.
    Islands / by Christine Webster.
      p. cm.—(Bridgestone books. Earthforms)
    Includes bibliographical references and index.
    ISBN 0-7368-3713-2 (hardcover)
    1. Islands—Juvenile literature. I. Title. II. Series.
GB471.W43 2005
910'.914'2—dc22   2004014277

Summary: Describes islands, including how they form, plants and animals on islands, how people and
      weather change islands, islands in North America, and Surtsey Island.

Editorial Credits
Becky Viaene, editor; Juliette Peters, designer; Anne McMullen, illustrator; Wanda Winch, photo
      researcher; Scott Thoms, photo editor

Photo Credits
Bruce Coleman Inc./Tony Arruza, 12
Corbis/Danny Lehman, cover
Corel, 1
Digital Vision/Gerry Ellis, 10
Folio Inc./Richard J. Quataert, 16
Image Ideas, Inc./Robert Houser, 6
James P. Rowan, 4, 8
Tom Stack & Associates Inc./Harold Simon, 18; M. Bradley, 14

1 2 3 4 5 6 10 09 08 07 06 05

Table of Contents

What Are Islands?

Islands are small pieces of land surrounded by water. Islands vary in size. Some islands are smaller than a city block. Greenland is one of the world's largest islands. It is about three times larger than the state of Texas.

Weather changes both big and small islands. Wind and waves can cause islands to form or disappear. Today, new islands continue to be discovered.

◄ Moku'ae'ae Island is about the size of five football fields. It is located off the Hawaiian island of Kauai.

How Do Islands Form?

Volcanoes form some islands. Hot **magma** boils deep in the earth. It bubbles up and out of a volcano as **lava**. Lava cools, hardens, and forms piles on the ocean floor. Islands form when the piles of lava stick out above the ocean. The Hawaiian Islands were formed this way.

Changes in water levels also make some islands. England was once connected to Europe. Now, the North Sea and English Channel separate it from Europe's mainland.

◄ Hot lava flows from a volcano. Islands form when lava cools in tall piles on the ocean floor.

Plants on Islands

The type of plants growing on islands depends on **climate**. Large, leafy palm trees grow on islands with hot, wet climates. Fewer plants can grow on islands with cold climates. Juniper trees with small leaves grow on islands with cold climates.

Islands formed by volcanoes start out with no plants. Over time, wind, water, and birds carried seeds to these islands. Coconut seeds were carried from the mainland to Hawaii. This plant still grows there today.

◄ Many large, leafy plants grow in Maui. This Hawaiian island has a hot, wet climate.

Animals on Islands

Often, animals on an island are found nowhere else in the world. Here they are safe from **predators** found on the mainlands.

Huge Galapagos tortoises only live on the Galapagos Islands, near Ecuador's mainland. On the mainland, rats and dogs would eat tortoise eggs.

The Komodo dragon lives on only a few islands. It swims between the islands, located off Asia's mainland. The large lizard's eggs are safe from pigs and dogs on these islands.

◀ Although Galapagos tortoises are large, they would not be protected from predators on the mainland.

Garden Key

Bush Key

Weather Changes Islands

Strong weather can change the shape of islands. Wind and waves **erode** islands. Wind blows sand away. Waves wash over sand and carry bits of it away to new areas. As they erode, islands get smaller.

Wind and waves can also push sand to a new place on the same island. Over time, the island changes shape. Wind can even join two nearby islands by blowing sand together.

◄ Sandy islands can change shape easily. Bush Key and Garden Key may someday be joined together by sand.

People Change Islands

People sometimes make major changes to islands. Trees are cut down so buildings can be put on islands. Without trees, soil erodes.

People also affect island wildlife. People often take boats to get to islands. Boats can dirty the water and soil. Plants and animals can't live in the dirty areas.

People sometimes bring new plants and animals to islands. This can harm an island's natural plants and animals. Today, few islands remain unchanged by people.

◀ People changed Garden Key when they built Fort Jefferson. The fort's walls now surround the island.

Islands in North America

North America has thousands of islands. Canada's Arctic Archipelago is a set of islands in the Arctic Ocean. The Arctic Archipelago is made up of more than 50 islands. Baffin Island is the largest. Many of these islands are covered with thick ice. No trees grow in these islands' cold climate.

Cozumel Island has a warm climate. Near Mexico's mainland, Cozumel Island is surrounded by the Caribbean Sea. Today, more than 75,000 people live on this island.

◀ Snow-covered mountains can be seen on Baffin Island. Less than 10,000 people live on this cold island.

Surtsey Island

In 1963, a volcano **erupted** under the ocean near Iceland. Magma rose from the floor of the ocean. It made the ocean boil and steam. Lava blasted to the surface.

In 1967, the lava blasts stopped. The lava had hardened into rock. A small island had formed. It was named Surtsey after the Icelandic god of fire. Surtsey Island covers about 1 square mile (3 square kilometers).

◄ Smoke rose from the volcano of Surtsey Island in 1963. The volcano has not erupted since 1967.

Pacific Ocean

N
W ←→ E
S

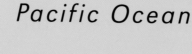

Kauai

Niihau

Oahu

Molokai

Maui

Lanai

Kahoolawe

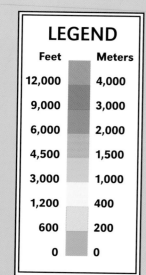

LEGEND

Feet		Meters
12,000		4,000
9,000		3,000
6,000		2,000
4,500		1,500
3,000		1,000
1,200		400
600		200
0		0

Hawaiian Islands

Hawaii

Islands on a Map

Islands are easy to find on maps. Look for tiny colored dots surrounded by blue water.

Elevation maps use different colors to show different elevations. Islands with steeply rising elevations were probably formed by volcanoes.

As islands change, new maps will continue to be made. Weather causes some islands to form and others to disappear.

◄ The steep rise in elevation helps show that volcanoes formed the Hawaiian Islands.

Glossary

climate (KLYE-mit)—the usual weather in a place

elevation (el-uh-VAY-shuhn)—the height above sea level; sea level is defined as zero elevation.

erode (i-RODE)—to wear away; wind and water erode soil and rock.

erupt (e-RUHPT)—to burst suddenly; a volcano shoots steam, lava, and ash into the air when it erupts.

lava (LAH-vuh)—the hot, liquid rock that pours out of a volcano when it erupts

magma (MAG-muh)—melted rock found beneath Earth's crust

predator (PRED-uh-tur)—an animal that hunts other animals for food

volcano (vol-KAY-noh)—a mountain with vents; lava, ash, and steam erupt out of vents.

Read More

Durbin, Christopher. *Islands.* Geography First. San Diego: Blackbirch Press, 2004.

Oxlade, Chris. *Islands.* Science Files: Earth. Milwaukee: Gareth Stevens, 2003.

Internet Sites

FactHound offers a safe, fun way to find Internet sites related to this book. All of the sites on FactHound have been researched by our staff.

Here's how:
1. Visit *www.facthound.com*
2. Type in this special code **0736837132** for age-appropriate sites. Or enter a search word related to this book for a more general search.
3. Click on the **Fetch It** button.

FactHound will fetch the best sites for you!

Index